4

The
Passion
of
Jesus

STUDIES FOR SMALL GROUPS • LEGACY...
Group
Study

Mark Moore
&
Jon Weece

International Standard Book Number 0-89900-823-2

TABLE
OF
CONTENTS

our behalf. At the same time, let's not minimize the fact that as children of a loving Father, our words do make a difference.

Lesson #4: Jesus prayed three times. If you thought the previous paragraph odd, this one will blow your mind. Jesus didn't settle accounts with God on the first round. It took three times before he marched resiliently to the enemy. It took three times before he resigned to God's will. Generally we don't like to talk this way since it dispels our "superhero" image of Jesus. Don't misunderstand, Jesus was God in the flesh, he walked on water, raised the dead, and was empowered by the Holy Spirit. At the same time, he was fully human. Never is that more clearly seen than in his garden prayers. He flat out wrestled with this decision. To pretend otherwise paints an unrealistic portrait of Jesus and sets up unrealistic demands of his followers. We too may come to God continually. We too may wrestle with his will for our lives. It's okay to have fears and doubts, even tears and pain. Your prayers are not perfect because you "worded them right" or "got it right the first time." Your prayers are perfect because they represent a real relationship with your heavenly Father. God doesn't expect you to "have it all together," he only asks that you be real and ultimately obey his directives for your life.

Pursuing the Passion of Jesus

1. Take with you and read *Too Busy Not to Pray* by Bill Hybels on your next vacation.
2. Determine a situation which you are facing which needs concentrated, committed prayer. Apply the four lessons from the text to this situation. If you do not have a serious circumstance in your life which needs such prayer, apply the lessons to the needs of a friend or something critical you have heard on the nightly news.

Eternity in the Balance

5   5

A KISS IN THE DARK

> The highest reward for man's toil is not what he gets for it, but what he becomes by it.
> —John Ruskin
>
> The pioneers are the guys with the arrows in their backs.
> —Erwin Potts

5   5

Text: Matthew 26:47-56; John 18:1-12   **Memory:** Matthew 26:52-54

Total Commitment   In 1964 a confrontation between Malaysia and Indonesia broke out on the island of Borneo.

A group of Gurkhas from Nepal were asked if they would be willing to jump from transport planes into combat against the Indonesians if the need arose. In the past the Gurkhas had been a fearless bunch, willing to do anything to win battles. But jumping from airplanes was a new concept to them. They discussed the idea with a British pilot who assured them that everything would be okay. The Gurkhas told the pilot they would jump, but only under the right conditions. The land had to be marshy or reasonably soft and they wanted the plane to fly no higher than 100 feet off the ground and at a very slow speed.

The British officers agreed that they could arrange for all

of their requests and still complete the military mission. The only exception was flying at a height of 100 feet. The British officer in charge explained to the Gurkhas that at 100 feet, they wouldn't have time to open their parachutes.

When the Gurkhas heard the officer say "parachutes," a confused look came over all of their faces. To the surprise of the British pilots, the Gurkhas had been willing to jump without the use of parachutes.

Commitment to a cause and courage often go hand in hand. Jesus embodied both and was willing to jump into a war zone without the help of conventional weapons of war.

Overview of the Text

Bad things often happen at night and the night seems to make bad things worse. Here Jesus hits rock bottom: betrayed by a friend, hated by a nation, abandoned by his disciples. Yet Jesus stands like a lighthouse in the midst of a dark and dangerous storm. He's not been moved from his mission. Even when he stands alone, he stands exceedingly tall.

Pondering the Passion of Jesus

✷ What battles in life have you had to fight on your own?

✷ Have there been times in your life when you've been abandoned or betrayed? How did you respond?

✷ What would you have done if you had seen Jesus put Malchus's ear back on his head?

✷ What do you think was going through the other disciples' minds as they watched the soldiers tie Jesus' hands behind his back?

Meaning of the Text

As the drama in the garden unfolds, several major players attempt to take center stage. We pick up the action at the gate. Jesus

A Kiss in the Dark

escorts the inner three from the interior of the garden to its entrance. There they join the other eight, as sleepy and dazed as the three. You do the math: one is missing.

Approaching fast and hard is a detachment of soldiers. John identifies them as a company, which would be 600 soldiers (John 18:3). Undoubtedly the eleven intuitively look to Jesus to see what their next move must be. This is the confrontation they have feared. The Chief Priests and Pilate joined forces. They come to arrest Jesus when he is most vulnerable. The crowds, loyal and eager, are tucked in bed on the other side of the Kidron. Jesus is outnumbered and certainly "outgunned." Their side has only three swords, the opposition is armed to the hilt with swords, clubs, shields, and torches. It doesn't look good.

The strangest thing happens, however. When the soldiers arrive, they just stand like statues. Nobody says a word until Jesus breaks the silence. "Who are you looking for?" He asks. "Jesus of Nazareth," comes the answer from somewhere in the crowd. With an ominous authority straight from the throne, Jesus simply says, "I am he!" You're not gonna believe what happens. The opposition falls to the ground! (John 18:6). When they get up and brush themselves off, they try to regain their composure. But they are still mute. Jesus, a second time, breaks the silence, "Who are you looking for?" Same question, same answer. This time Jesus replies, "If you're looking for me, then let these men go." How amazing that in Jesus' crucible hour, he is still thinking of those he loves. This will not change, even on the cross.

At this point, the first major player steps out of the shadows into the limelight. The eleven rub their eyes in disbelief. What's *he* doing with *them*? Could it possibly be that Judas would eat a meal of fidelity, receive the washing of feet, feign loyalty for three years, and turn traitor so late in the game? They stand paralyzed—all but Jesus. He says, "Judas, are you betraying the Son of Man with a kiss? (Luke 22:48). Friend, do

what you came for" (Matt. 26:50). Believe it or not, he did!
You know what's really crazy about this? *He didn't even have to!* Jesus had already marked himself. Judas' sign was now irrelevant (unless, of course, the high priest believed one of his men was going to take the fall for him as an impostor). Nevertheless, the guards dutifully grab Jesus' arms and begin to bind them behind his back.

A second player takes center stage. He's wielding the butcher knife used earlier to carve the Passover Lamb. His name is Peter. He lashes out at the nearest victim. He happens to be a man named Malchus. He was the High Priest's personal assistant. A sword flashes across the light of a torch. A man screams, clutching his ear. It happened so fast in the shadows that few were sure what actually happened. Malchus's screams undoubtedly clarified quickly the assault. With blood streaming through his fingers he yelps, "He cut off my ear! That Galilean just cut off my ear!" Jesus pulls his hands away from the guards and reaches to the dirt to retrieve the wayward appendage. He then proceeds to snap it back on like a Lego block. The crowd is once again silent. Jesus once again breaks the silence and orders Peter to stand down. He does. In fact, Peter ran into the night. The others followed. It's not that Peter's a coward. After all, anyone with enough Chutzpah to attack a trained company of soldiers when outnumbered 60 to 1 can hardly be classified as a coward! No, the real issue was Peter only knew how to fight with a sword—he knows nothing of spiritual warfare. Once Jesus strips him of his only armament, he runs off, defenseless and scared. Peter was ready to defend Jesus, until he realized Jesus wasn't even going to defend himself.

Jesus is now alone; very much alone. A third player comes center stage. Well, they actually come as a pair (Luke 22:52). They are the chief priests, specifically Annas and Caiaphas. They likely turned to the Romans as well as to Judas and said something to the effect of, "We'll take it from here." They knew exactly what had to be done: A brief trial, a transfer to Pilate, an execution. It shouldn't take long . . . all the arrangements have already been made.

It really does look like they are driving the events from here on out. Jesus concedes, "This is your hour—when darkness reigns" (Luke 22:53). "But this has all taken place that the writings of the prophets might be fulfilled" (Matt. 26:56). Sure, they were in charge, but only because their hour of darkness was ordained by God. The man of sorrows is whisked away and his trials begin.

So what is the point of the story? What are we to learn? Two things, I think. First, Jesus was very much alone at his arrest. One of his own men betrayed him, the leaders of the nation were against him, the Governor sent troops to arrest him, and even his chosen band abandoned him. *No one* stood by his side. In fact, there is a strange story in Mark about a young man who fled the scene naked, leaving his cloak in the clutch of a soldier (Mark 14:51-52). Granted, it's an odd tale that is likely autobiographical. Yet it paints a picture of utter abandonment. That is, one young man even left his clothes behind to get away from this man. Socially Jesus is as naked as our anonymous streaker. That he was abandoned heightened his passion. Not only was his suffering immense, it was exacerbated by utter aloneness.

And yet (this is the second lesson), he was still in total control. Once Jesus yielded to God in prayer, there was no external control of his life. All three players who attempted to usurp his centrality found themselves rebuffed. Judas tried to hog the limelight, but Jesus subverted his plan. Jesus identified himself while Judas was still in the shadows. His betrayal was really unnecessary. Then along came Peter. He was going to swoop in and save the day. His valor would certainly save the Master . . . yeah, right! Jesus wound up saving Malchus (and Peter); Peter wound up running scared. His efforts at bravery were foolish and inane. Finally, along came the chief priests.

With a false air of authority they brush all the others aside—
until Jesus puts them in their place. Far from being in control,
they are the ones driven by prophecy and driven to their ulti-
mate demise for rejecting the Son of God.

This powerful trilogy professes the greatness of Jesus.
Even in his crucible hour, when left all alone, he alone is in
control. He cannot be captured, overpowered, outwitted, or
undone. Again, he is the incomparable Christ!

Pursuing the Passion of Jesus

Take a sheet of notebook paper and draw a line down the middle. At the
top of one column write "successes" and at the top of the second column
write "failures." Read through Matthew 14–20. List the disciples' successes
and failures (especially Peter's). Put an asterisk (*) by those items that
remind you of yourself. When you finish listing these highs and lows, read
John 21.

A Kiss in the Dark

6   6

"HIS OWN RECEIVED HIM NOT"

6   6

> It is better to risk saving a guilty man than to condemn an innocent one.
>
> —Voltaire

Text: Matthew 26:57-68; John 18:19-24   **Memory:** Matthew 26:64

Is This Justice? With 70 percent of the world's lawyers practicing in America, one might think justice would prevail. That's not always the case.

A burglar recently fell through a skylight while robbing a school. His attorneys charged the school with negligence and won $260,000 in damages. A man in Massachusetts stole a car from a parking lot, then died in a traffic accident. His family sued the parking lot for letting him steal the car. In San Francisco a cab driver corralled a mugger by pinning him to a wall with his taxi. The thief ended up with a broken leg, so a jury ordered the cabby to pay the crook $24,595 for using excessive force. One lady claimed she lost her psychic powers after being injected with dye during a CAT scan. She was awarded nearly a million dollars in damages. Charles Colson says, "One wonders why she didn't foresee her problems and avoid the scan altogether."

If these breaches of justice frustrate you, then what takes place in the next few chapters just might send you over the edge.

Overview of the Text

Metal is best tested by heating it to its melting point. Jesus is now thrown into the furnace. He stands alone to face his accusers. They are vehement, vicious, and deceitful. Like piranhas attacking their prey, they nip at Jesus in frenzied forays. This is hardly the epitome of a calm courtroom. People are scurrying in and out. Information is whispered in the high priest's ear even as another false accuser blurts out charges he cannot confirm. In a noisy atmosphere of hate and deceit, Jesus stands calmly—too calmly. His silence paves the way for his execution. This first phase of Jesus' trial will take place under the auspices of the Jewish court. He stands before the pillars of Israel as a native son gone bad.

Pondering the Passion of Jesus

✷ Have you ever experienced injustice in your life? How did you respond?
✷ If you could remove one crime from the world today, what crime would it be?
✷ If you were a judge, how would you treat the "accused" in your courtroom?

Meaning of the Text

Jesus first faces Annas, the former high priest, deposed by the Romans some twenty years prior. Nevertheless, his clout was still thick among his countrymen, particularly since the Mosaic law ordained a high priest for life. Annas still had the chief voice in the nation. Moreover, he could buy a bit of time for his son-in-law Caiaphas, who was currently Rome's appointed high priest. Annas stalls while Caiaphas orchestrates a kangaroo court.

"His Own Received Him Not"

There was really only one question Annas asked: "What do you teach?" It was a stupid question which Jesus answers appropriately. "I've been teaching publicly in *your* temple. Why don't you ask those who heard me?!" All of a sudden some big ol' bruiser claps Jesus upside the head. "What was that for?" he demanded. "Tell me what I've said that was illegal or else tell me why you just broke the law to strike me." To this day that question has gone unanswered. This incident illustrates just how far afield the legality of this trial would go. You can't go around slapping prisoners. For that matter you're not supposed to have a trial in the middle of the night. Nor are you supposed to allow contradictory witnesses or allow the High Priest to determine the verdict through strong-arm tactics. But then again, these are desperate times that require desperate measures.

Caiaphas is now prepared to interrogate the Galilean. So Jesus is whisked over to see him, likely in a separate wing of the same royal palace. The first accusation against Jesus flies from the lips of several false witnesses. "He threatened to destroy our temple," they say, "and raise it up again in three days." This hearkens back to the first time Jesus cleansed the temple some three years earlier (cf. John 2:19). Jesus, of course, was talking about his own body, not bricks and mortar. Thus, these words are no real threat to the temple.

However, that doesn't mean that Jesus never threatened the temple. One thinks immediately of Matthew 24, where Jesus predicts its fall within that very generation. Between 66–70 A.D. the Romans did, in fact march on the city, tear down the walls, and burn the temple. Jesus' words were fulfilled to the letter. Of course, Matthew 24 was a private discussion with the twelve, not likely something that would come up at a public trial just 2 ½ days later. However, there were other statements of Jesus that would have correctly been interpreted as threats to the temple. For example, twice Jesus weeps over the city with these words: "O Jerusalem, Jerusalem, you who kill the prophets and

stone those sent to you, how often I have longed to gather your
children together, as a hen gathers her chicks under her wings,
but you were not willing. Look, your house is left to you deso-
late" (Matt. 23:37; Luke 13:34). Again, during the cleansing of
the temple, Jesus combined two prophecies: "My house is to be
a house of prayer" (Isa. 56:7), "But you have made it a den of
robbers" (Jer. 7:11). Both texts, read in their contexts, are overt
threats to the temple and its leaders.

   Jesus never came out and said, "You kill me and I'll
destroy your temple." Nevertheless, there were public intima-
tions that Jesus' death would bring ill-fate to the Holy Place.
The charge that Jesus threatened the temple was actually
true, it just wasn't something they could prove. That must
have been infuriating for Caiaphas. So he introduces a second
charge—blasphemy. "This man blasphemes God by claiming
equality with him." While Jesus never slandered God overtly,
to claim divine status would bring Yahweh down to man's
level. At least that was the thinking of the High Priest. He
didn't even consider Jesus a *good* man, let alone *God's* man.

   Yet Caiaphas has the same problem with this second
accusation as he did with the first. He knows it's true, he just
can't prove it. Therefore, he up and asks Jesus point blank,
"Are you the Son of God?" To this the Master replies, "It is as
you say" (which must have irked him considerably). "In the
future you will see the Son of Man sitting at the right hand of
the Mighty One and coming on the clouds of heaven."
Obviously, Caiaphas is not going to like this. But it gets worse
the deeper you look. This is an allusion to Psalm 110:1, which
claims divine privileges for the High Priest, Melchizedek.
More than that, verse two is a direct threat to the religious
hierarchy who stands in his way. Jesus could hardly have
chosen a text that was more offensive and confrontational. In
other words, the High Priest asks him to convict himself. He
does. But not without a bit of biting critique. Jesus threatens
Caiaphas with the destruction due God's enemies.

"His Own Received Him Not"

42   At this Caiaphas tears his robe and begins to squall, "Blasphemer, blasphemer. You all heard him! What should we do with such a villain? Don't you agree that he deserves to die?!" The hirelings, of course, concur. Jesus' fate is sealed in the Sanhedrin.

Because Jesus was destined to die, he's now treated as a condemned felon. They play a game with him which was somewhat like blind-man's bluff. The soldiers cover his eyes, and take turns punching him in the face. They then challenge him to prophesy which one(s) hit him. When he remains silent, they give him another opportunity to "redeem" himself. Over and over they played this game until Isaiah 52:14 was fulfilled, "There were many who were appalled at him—his appearance was so disfigured beyond that of any man and his form marred beyond human likeness."

And so it begins. The man of sorrows endures the suffering we deserved. He took upon himself the penalty due a wayward world. By his stripes we were healed. You know what is really kind of strange? Both accusations they made were true. Jesus did threaten the temple at their rejection, and he did claim to be God's envoy. If Jesus wasn't who he claimed, he did, indeed, deserve to die, according to the Mosaic law. If, however, he is who he claimed, they are about to make a galactic mistake!

Pursuing the Passion of Jesus

Rent the movie *The Green Mile*. Before you watch it, read Matthew 26:57-68 and John 18:19-24. Take note of all the Christ themes in the main character.

7   7

ON THE ANVIL OF ROME

7   7

> The whole art of government consists in being honest.
>
> —Thomas Jefferson
>
> It's an awful thing to be President of the United States. It means giving up nearly everything one holds dear.
>
> —Woodrow Wilson

Text: John 18:28–19:15   **Memory:** John 18:36-37

The Power of Martyrdom

When Joseph Ton was a pastor in Romania he was arrested by the secret police for publishing a sermon calling for the churches to refuse to submit to the communist government's demand for control over their ministries. When an official told him he must renounce his sermon, he replied, "No sir! I won't do that!"

The official, surprised that anyone would respond so forcefully to the secret police, said, "Aren't you aware that I can use force against you?"

"Sir, let me explain this to you," Ton said. "You see, your supreme weapon is killing. My supreme weapon is dying. . . . You know that my sermons are spread all over the country on tapes. When you kill me, I only sprinkle them with my blood. They will speak 10 times louder after that. So go on, sir, kill me. When you kill me, I win the supreme victory."

In this chapter, you'll see that Jesus recognized the limitations of Pilate's authority and embraced the potential of his death.

Overview of the Text

Due to a surreal set of circumstances, Jesus passes through Pilate's diary. Had it not been for Rome's recent decision to strip the Jewish nation of the right to capital punishment, Pilate never would have met him. But there he stands, this peasant with no real status nor any real charges against him. Pilate's inexplicable concern for justice, his relentless attempts to release the Nazarene, are surely a credit to his character. Yet it's not enough to erase this indelible blemish on his biography. Indeed, it appears that Pilate has the power of life and death over Jesus. Yet nothing could be further from the truth. He who is in chains bears God's scepter of justice. History betrays the truth of this encounter: It was Jesus who determined Pilate's destiny, not the other way around. Pilate's cowardice, now dripping from recently washed hands, determines what history would remember of this ignoble man.

Pondering the Passion of Jesus

- Why do you think Pilate so desperately wanted to release Jesus? Trace some of the thoughts that would be racing through *your* mind had you been in his shoes.
- What part of Jesus' suffering and beatings impresses you the most? Could you have endured such mistreatment in silence?

Meaning of the Text

The thunder clouds form as the angry escort throws Jesus on Pilate's palatial doorstep. They ask for an execution without so much as offering any accusation. When Pilate demands an explanation they try to intimidate him by shouting, "If he were not a criminal we would not have handed him over to you." While the Jewish leaders will ultimately succeed in forcing Pilate's judicial hand, he's going to make them work at it. He demands a legal charge; they level three (cf. Luke 23:2): He subverts the nation, refuses to pay taxes, and claims to be king. The first two are simply bogus. He neither evades taxes nor causes riots (except for those uncomfortable encounters when the Pharisees get out of sorts). But this third charge the governor cannot afford to ignore. You see, anyone in the Roman Empire that claimed to be king would inevitably encounter the cold steel of Caesar's retribution. Notice, this is where Pilate's investigation begins.

"So you claim to be a king?" he asks. Jesus responds, "Is that your idea or the Sanhedrin's?" Oh my, you should have been there. Pilate got all bent out of shape. Such insolence, from a peasant no less! Actually, Jesus isn't being snippy, he's trying to clarify his own answer. You see, if Pilate is asking if Jesus were a rival to Rome, the answer is clearly, "No." If he's asking whether he was the rightful leader of the Jewish nation, the answer is "absolutely." Jesus' explanation (John 18:36-38) leaves Pilate perplexed about Jesus but clear concerning the charges: This man is not a criminal deserving of death.

He goes out to the angry mob and announces his decision to dismiss the case. This, of course, sent them into a frenzied dither of venomous accusations. Jesus stands in stoic silence. Pilate watches incredulously (Matt. 27:12-14). He wanted, in the worst way, to let him go, but Jesus isn't helping him out.

In the midst of their foray, someone said, "His heresy started in Galilee and has slithered all the way up here!" "Now wait just a minute" Pilate thought, "He's from Galilee and that's Herod's jurisdiction, not mine." That's good news. Better news: Pilate had been at odds with Herod and Herod had been trying to track down Jesus. This is just the kind of thing that could be played to Pilate's advantage (Luke 23:6-8,

On the Anvil of Rome

12). Best news: Herod was in town for the Passover celebration. Hence, Jesus was expeditiously transferred to the usurper of the Jewish throne.

Now here's an interesting encounter. The king of the Jews meets the King of the Jews. Herod cynically invites Jesus to do a miracle, to prove his claim to rival his throne. Not only would he not honor the request, Jesus wouldn't even talk to him even though Herod drilled him with questions. Fascinating! The only person Jesus refused to talk to in all the Gospels was the king of the Jews. The embittered king gave leave to his guards to repay the insult. They dressed him in a purple robe in mock coronation and spit in his face. With this regal robe and spit encrusted in his beard they returned him to the governor.

Pilate, to be sure, was none too happy to see him again. This guy just keeps coming back. (He has no idea!) The governor attempts again to release him. The fact is, Pilate tried no less than ten times, according to a harmony of all four Gospel accounts, to release Jesus in a variety of ways. Where mere words won't work, he attempts to bribe them. Each year at Passover, the governor demonstrated his "magnanimous grace" by releasing a prisoner of their choosing (cf. Mark 16:6-10). This goodwill gesture delighted the locals. This year he gave them a choice between two men of *his* choosing. The first, of course was Jesus. The second was some notorious (or famous, depending which side you were one) rebel. His name was Barabbas. He was a known thief and assassin. Now, given the choice between a savage renegade or this magician/prophet, Pilate was sure they would choose the latter. Not so. They shouted to the high heavens for the bloody thief. "So what shall I do with Jesus?" he asked. As with a single voice the crowd cried, "Crucify him!" Let those words reverberate from the page: "Crucify him!" For what? Because he placed children on his knee? Because he had raised a widow's son? Or perhaps because he said such horrible things as,

The Passion of Jesus

"Pray for those who persecute you"? Clearly, this event is driven not merely by the selfishness of men, nor even by the schemes of the Devil, but by the very hand of the sovereign God.

About that time Pilate's wife came out to the judgment seat (Matt. 27:19-21). Considering that wives were supposed to keep to the private sectors of the home, this is a striking appearance. Well, her business is urgent—she had a dream. This seems strange to us. But to Pilate (or any Mediterranean person for that matter), dreams were not to be taken lightly. These were communiqués from the gods. Pilate can't help but take this seriously. Jesus told him that he had no power except what was given him by God. Now his own wife is saying that the divine has his eye on these events. His concern now gives way to quivering.

In one last ditch effort he reiterates Jesus' innocence and offers to have him flogged and then released. This particular punishment was one of the most despicable and feared tortures of the ancient world. It was generally carried out by two guards. They stood on either side of the victim who would be tied to a pillar or hung from a ring on the wall. Each wielded a whip of sorts. It was a long-handled stick with a bunch of leather strands attached to one end. These strands were knotted with sharp objects: bone, glass, metal. The two most common kinds were the knuckle bones of sheep and paired lead balls. The victim would be stripped and each guard would take turns slapping the sharp objects against the raw flesh from the shoulders down to the calves. After the whip made contact with the skin, the soldier would then pull down sharply, raking the victim's flesh. The first few blows would yield welts that eventually burst. Before long the flogging left flayed strips of muscle dangling loosely from the bones. The vertebrae were invariably exposed to the open air and many men were blinded as the sharp objects reached around and gouged out there eyes. Sixty percent of the victims died from

On the Anvil of Rome

the scourging, sometimes from loss of blood, sometimes because there wasn't enough flesh to hold in their intestines. This was truly cruel and unusual punishment.

One last time Pilate brings the bloodied spectacle out to the people. He declares, "I find no basis for a charge against him." They replied, "If you let this man go, you are no friend of Caesar." And that was the linchpin. Because of the desire to save his own precarious political career, Pilate yielded to their request lest they send to Rome an unfavorable report that would get him deposed. He washed his hands and turned his back on the Savior of the world.

Oddly, within three years Pilate would be called to Rome and banished to Gaul. That's right, he sold out the Son of God for a petty political career that would last not more than 36 months. Oh, don't be too hard on the guy. Some of us have sold out for much less.

Pursuing the Passion of Jesus

John Wycliffe, a 14th century preacher, helped translate the Bible into English so that it could be accessible to every believer of his era. After completing the task, he wrote, "This Bible is translated and shall make possible a government of the people, by the people, and for the people." Find a copy of Abraham Lincoln's "Gettysburg Address" and compare Wycliffe's words with those of President Lincoln. In the comparison, you'll find "cross" themes.

8   8

TWO HEADS HANGING— BY SHAME AND BY ROPE

8   8

> Whenever you fall,
> pick up something.
> —Oswald Avery
>
> I have more trouble
> with D.L. Moody than
> any other man I know.
> —D.L. Moody

Text: Matthew 26:69–27:10   **Memory:** Matthew 26:75

The Power of Forgiveness   The picture haunted him. Like many Americans, John Plummer, minister of Bethany United Methodist Church in Purcellville, Virginia, was moved by the Vietnam-era Pulitzer-prize-winning photo of 9-year-old Phan Thi Kim Phuc, naked and horribly burned, running from a napalm attack.

But for Plummer the picture had special significance. In 1972 he was responsible for setting up the air strike on the village of Trang Bang—a strike approved after he twice assured there were no civilians in the area.

After becoming a Christian in 1990, Plummer felt called to the ministry and attended seminary. In June 1996 he learned that Kim Phuc was still alive and living in Toronto. The next month he attended a military reunion and met someone who knew both Kim Phuc and the photographer.

50 Plummer learned that on that fateful day in 1972, Kim Phuc and her family were hiding in a pagoda in Trang Bang when a bomb hit the building. Kim Phuc and others ran into the street, where they were hit by napalm being dropped from another plane. She tore off her burning clothing as she fled. Two of her cousins were killed.

The photographer and other journalists poured water from canteens on her burns. She collapsed moments after the famous photo and was rushed by car to a hospital. The girl spent fourteen months in hospitals and was operated on by a San Francisco plastic surgeon.

Plummer learned that Kim Phuc was speaking in Washington, D.C. He went and heard Kim Phuc say that if she ever met the pilot of the plane, she would tell him she forgives him and that they cannot change the past, but she hoped they could work together in the future.

Plummer was able to get word to Kim Phuc that the man she wanted to meet was there.

"She saw my grief, my pain, my sorrow," Plummer said. "She held out her arms to me and embraced me. All I could say was, 'I'm sorry; I'm sorry; I'm sorry' over and over again. At the same time she was saying, 'It's all right; It's all right; I forgive; I forgive.'"

Overview of the Text

While Jesus was on trial in the palace of the High Priest, both Peter and Judas were on trial outside. All three trials are going badly, and for very different reasons. The text deliberately juxtaposes these two Apostles on either side of Jesus' condemnation by the high priest. They're not tethered together because they are so much alike but because they are so different. This is a study in contrasts. Oh, to be sure, both turned their backs on Jesus, both were even identified with Satan (Matt. 16:23; Luke 22:3; John 13:27), and both felt terrible for what they had done. Nonetheless, they are miles apart in motive, purpose, and consequence. Judas is the model

The Passion of Jesus

"antichrist." He could make a great case for his own authenticity. Yet his heart reeks of unbelief, one so dark it bears the shadows of God's foreordained plan. Peter, on the other hand, is the quintessential disciple who blunders along with good intentions but is plagued with poor decisions. He is a mirror we look into through heavy tears, the kind only produced by deeply embarrassing failure. Somehow through the looking glass Peter smiles back at us in knowing recollection. His countenance says, "It will be okay . . . after three days."

Pondering the Passion of Jesus

* If you can bring yourself to engage in such open self-disclosure, tell of a time that you felt like Peter in the courtyard. What did Jesus do to bring you back into his open fellowship?
* What makes the difference between a Judas and a Peter? How can one know which path they are treading?
* What sin in your life are you currently carrying that needs to be forgiven?

Meaning of the Text

Peter had been so bold, so confident. Even when Jesus predicted his denial Peter all but called him a liar. He wasn't just idly boasting either. Remember Malchus? Peter pulled out one of the butcher knives they'd used on the Passover lamb and took his best shot. I can assure you Peter wasn't aiming for his ear! He was trying to give him a hair cut at the collar bone. Malchus just happened to be a quick little fellow . . . almost quick enough to avoid the blade altogether. Now if Peter is willing to take on 600 armed soldiers with but two swords among the twelve you can hardly call him a coward. Peter was telling the truth when he said, "Lord, I'm willing to die with you." Yet poor Peter winds up running off into the night when Jesus took away his sword. After all, he didn't know how to fight with weapons of spiritual warfare yet.

Two Heads Hanging

52   He may have disappeared quickly, but he didn't go far. He and John can't bring themselves to lose sight of the Master. They followed the posse to the palace of the high priest. John had some connections with the family. We don't know just what they were but they were significant enough to gain him access to the courtyard. He went and got Peter a "backstage pass." That's when the trouble began. I don't know what Peter's thinking, but I suspect it has something to do with figuring out how to free Jesus through some special forces op.

Each of the four Gospels describe the scene differently. That's not surprising. Things are moving quickly, few know what's really going on, and it is dark. Moreover, John and Peter are the only eyewitnesses to these events, and I doubt Peter was too eager to talk about it. Nonetheless, our reconstruction looks something like this. As Peter passed through the gate, a servant girl recognized him. Her job was to watch the gate and sound the alarm (i.e., scream like a school girl), if something was awry. When she saw him she said, "Hey, wait a minute, aren't you one of the Galileans? Weren't you with Jesus?" "NO!" Peter protests. "I don't know what you're talking about . . . *you* don't know what you're talking about." Because little girls have little clout he can brush her aside and head on into the courtyard. There he finds a charcoal fire. Sitting around it are soldiers swapping stories of their heroic capture. Peter stands at the perimeter listening intently, catching the secondhand warmth from the embers. It was all he could do not to shout, "That's not the way it happened and you know it!" But subversives like Peter learn to listen intently and talk sparsely.

His face is dimly lit; his eyes are inflamed. The girl at the gate studies him. Catching what she can from the flickering torches and orange glow of the braziers, it takes her the better part of the hour to put it all together. Finally she is confident enough to cross over into the men's territory and identify Peter as the Galilean rebel. Every head turns and Peter stands as a sheep among wolves. He lies; he swears on an oath; and he excuses himself to the shadows of the gate. There it is less crowded but no more private. Now all the courtyard is buzzing and pointing in his direction. After several conferences a group of men concur that it is, in fact Peter. One of Malchus's own relatives was the linchpin. A delegation approaches Peter to get his confession. What they got was a loud and boisterous oath of denial.

At that very moment two things happened. First, a cock crowed—not so unusual but his timing was impeccable. With two shrill cries beckoning the dawn, Peter's whole world was plunged into dark despair. Second, Jesus peered through the door and locked eyes with his chief Apostle. It must have been one of those knowing, forlorn looks—the kind of gaze that comes only in the briefest moments that mark you for a lifetime. Peter ran into the dark, distraught.

Push fast forward—not too far—somewhere between Caiaphas's trial and Jesus' transfer to Pilate. The reality of Jesus' conviction awakened Iscariot from his satanic spell, and he realized what he had done (even if he was yet ignorant of to whom he had done it). He returns his ill-gotten gain to the Chief Priests and Elders. He's full of remorse; they are not. In their piety they paradoxically refuse to touch his tainted money. The enormity of their hypocrisy is astounding! In furious vengeance Judas marches into the Holy Place and scatters the blood money amidst the droplets from bulls and goats. It was a scandalous, heinous act in a soon-to-be defunct temple that no longer housed either the ark or the Shekinah glory of God. Such desecration deserves death which Judas is about to self-inflict.

He goes out to a barren field, which overlooks the valley of Gehenna, which yields nothing but clay for potters. From there he looked across the old city of David to the crowning glory of the temple on the north. He tied a rope to a not-so-

Two Heads Hanging

sturdy branch. With his last breath he took in the stench of the burning refuse in the valley below. With trembling hands he secured the noose and added to the legendary horror of that place by taking his own life. Interestingly, Luke adds a gory detail that Judas fell down the slopes spilling his intestines as he tumbled (Acts 1:18). A likely scenario is this: He hung there unnoticed all day Friday and through the Sabbath rest the next day. By Sunday morning his body was bloated and the earthquake that opened Jesus' tomb also dislodged the branch, sending his spewing body across the crags to the burning refuse below where it belonged.

Thus is the saga of the defection of two most prominent Apostles. They are, in many ways, so much alike. Both were leaders of the band. Both were, at one time, identified with Satan (Matt. 16:23; Luke 22:3; John 13:27). Both were in Jesus' inner circle and privy to private teaching. Both abandoned Jesus and both felt terrible about what they had done. While the surface similarities are striking, the difference between Peter and Judas are colossal:

Peter	Judas
Followed Jesus into the courtyard	Left Jesus at the Communion Meal
Sought to effect an escape	Delivered him into his enemies' hands
Acted impetuously under pressure	Premeditated his betrayal unto assassination
Denied knowing Jesus to save himself	Betrayed him for financial gain
Jesus predicted his restitution	Jesus predicted his ultimate demise
He repented (John 21:15-19)	He merely felt sorry (*metamelomai*) (Matt. 27:3)

Because of these pronounced differences, Peter was destined to sit on one of the twelve thrones (Matt. 19:28) while Iscariot was damned to destruction (John 17:12). How can two people look so much alike on the surface—even act in such similar ways—and yet have such different destinies? It comes down to this one simple, telling thing: Love. Do you remember the question Jesus asked Peter at his restitution? His relentless trilogy: "Do you love me? . . . Do you love me? . . . Do you love me?" Peter's answer rang back each time "YES, YES, YES!"

Peter really did love Jesus. Iscariot did not. We can wrestle all we want with the sovereignty of God vs. the free will of these two men. But the bottom line is that our eternal destiny rests in a relationship with Jesus, a relationship of love. Failures in the courtyard are not what keep people out of heaven; it's their lack of love in the divorce court. It's not our track record that gets us into heaven but our wedding ring.

Pursuing the Passion of Jesus

Write a letter to someone you've hurt asking for forgiveness. Write a second letter to someone who's waiting to hear you say, "I forgive you for what you've done."

Two Heads Hanging

9   9

THE DEATH OF LIFE

> To be crucified means, first, the man on the cross is facing only one direction; second, he is not going back; and third, he has no further plans of his own.
>
> —A.W. Tozer

9   9

Text: John 19:18   Memory: 1 Corinthians 5:21

One Life for Many In May of 1946 in a tucked away corner of the earth called Los Alamos, a young and daring scientist was carrying out a necessary experiment in preparation for the atomic test to be conducted in the waters of the South Pacific atoll at Bikini.

He had successfully performed such an experiment many times before. In his effort to determine the amount of U-235 necessary for a chain reaction—scientists call it the critical mass—he would push two hemispheres of uranium together. Then, just as the mass became critical, he would push them apart with his screwdriver, thus instantly stopping the chain reaction.

But that day, just as the material became critical, the screwdriver slipped. The hemispheres of uranium came too close together. Instantly the room was filled with a dazzling bluish haze. Young Louis Slotin, instead of ducking and thereby possibly saving himself, tore the two hemispheres apart with his hands and thus interrupted the chain reaction.

In a daring move, Slotin saved the lives of seven other people in the laboratory. As he waited for the car that was to take them to the hospital, he said quietly and reassuringly to a friend, "You'll come through all right. But I haven't the faintest chance myself." Nine days later, his prediction came to pass and he died.

Two thousand years ago, Jesus walked into a heavily contaminated environment, allowing himself to be tainted by its sin, so that its chain reaction would be broken and we could live free from its curse.

Overview of the Text

It is such a short sentence . . . such a simple statement, yet these three words reverberate across time and shake the very foundations of civilization: "They crucified him." In a sense it is shocking that such a ponderous fact should be captured in just three words. Surely there's more to say, surely some explanation is needed. Well, that's true, but we should bear in mind that by the time the Gospels were written the message of Jesus' resurrection had already fanned into flame a considerable army of believers. Their punctuation was on Jesus' life, not his death. Furthermore, to simply say, "They crucified him," was certainly enough of an explanation to an eyewitness of this heinous torture. Remember, there were no air bags to protect them from the harsh realities of subsistence life in an occupied land. It is we, not they, who need an explanation of these three short words. To that end we now turn.

Pondering the Passion of Jesus

✵ Historically, what thoughts would have come to mind when Jesus talked to his countrymen about crucifixion? How is this different from the thoughts

The Death of Life

that would pass through the minds of Christians in Paul's congregations?

- How has the cross been misconstrued in people's minds today?
- Why is it so essential that we take up a cross to follow Jesus? How is it that this acceptance of death breathes life into the believer?

Meaning of the Text

It is strange, indeed, that the cross ever became a symbol of Christianity. After all, we had many "nice" pictures to draw from. For many years the fish was used because its name in Greek cryptically represented "Jesus Christ, God, Son, Savior." The early Christians in the catacombs loved the picture of a shepherd with a lamb strewn across his shoulders. That would have been nice. The peace dove representing the Holy Spirit would make dandy letterhead. So why did we have to choose a bloodied beam of wood?

At a church in Georgia recently, a preacher gave a famous author a tour of the building. With pride the minister pointed to the imported pews and luxurious decorations. As they wrapped up the tour, the two of them stepped outside into the darkness of night. A spotlight shone on a huge cross atop the steeple.

"That cross alone cost us ten thousand dollars," the minister said with a satisfied smile.

The distinguished author said, "You were cheated. Times were when Christians could get them for free."

This may come as a surprise to you, but this symbol was not popularized until the fourth century *after* crucifixion was made illegal as a form of punishment. Before that it truly was too barbaric, vicious, and cruel to depict anyone's faith. In other words, as long as it was still seen, its sting was too real to be palatable as a religious symbol.

Crucifixion was "invented" by the Persians some 400 years before Christ. Originally they simply stuck a wooden

beam in the ground and sharpened the top end of it. They
pulled the victim spread eagle by all four limbs and held his
sternum just above the point. They then allowed his feet to
drop so he was at about a 60° angle and they jerked down far
enough that the point protruded up through the throat. While
this is an effective method of execution as well as a poignant
deterrent to other would-be felons, the Romans found that it
disposed of the victim far too quickly. They discovered that
nailing a person to a beam, rather than impaling them on it,
kept them alive for days. In fact, the average victim of crucifixion survived on the cross for three days (the longest
recorded was seven).

The Romans began experimenting with various methods
of nailing to maximize the pain of punishment. They found
that a nail positioned between the two bones of the forearm
(the radius and ulna), and just behind the complex of wrist
bones, would secure the victim to the cross without causing
a fatal injury. An added benefit was the fact that such a pierc-
ing would sever the median nerve, shooting searing pain up
through the arms clear to the shoulder blades. Furthermore,
it would cause the fingers and hand to curl inward in a tight
contraction like the claws of a bird.

Next the feet were affixed to the stipes (the vertical beam
of the cross). It is most common for portraits of Jesus to have
his feet nailed together at the front of the cross with one nail.
This is almost certainly inaccurate. Archaeologists have
found only one skeletal remains of a crucifixion victim. You
might say, "What? Why only one, weren't there thousands?"
Well yes, and most of them were left to rot or thrown to wild
dogs. Few were buried in secure coffins. Besides, the nails
were always retrieved so it is actually quite fortunate that we
even have one. This guy's name was Johannan (at least that
was the name inscribed on the top of his coffin). Apparently
he was crucified on an olive wood cross and the nail, which
passed through his right calcaneus (heel) hit a knot in the

60 olive wood and curled backward. This "hook" brought with it a chunk of the wood and smashed it against Johannan's heel. The nail was simply too much trouble to retrieve and now worthless anyway, so they left it in.

Now, there are two things interesting about this whole scenario. First, the nail was only about 4 ½ inches long—far too short to pass through both feet and embed in the cross. Second, it passed through the *side* of the heel, not the top of the foot. Thus both feet were nailed independently to the side of the cross, or twisted 90° from the torso and both nailed independently to the front of the cross. Either way, the nails would send the same kind of agony up through the pelvic area as the ones in the wrists sent through the shoulders.

There the victim hung, usually about 18 inches off the ground, supported by nothing but the four focal points of pain (save one small block of wood strategically placed to aggravate the tail bone). Stripped of all dignity and hanging by a thin thread to life, they were left to die. Question: What killed a victim of crucifixion? The most common answer is "suffocation." This may have, at times been true, but certainly wasn't in the case of Jesus. This notion was popularized by a French physician named Pierre Barbet who noted that men hung by their hands in WWII died quickly because they soon lost the strength to pull themselves up for a gulp of air. He thus postulated that crucifixion victims died because they soon lost the strength to pull themselves up to breathe. However, another physician named Frederick Zugibe noticed that victims of crucifixion were not hung with their hands above their heads but out to the side. He had some volunteers come to his laboratory and tied them up in a similar manner to those who would have been crucified. He monitored their breathing, and while it was labored, it was not lethal. This also accords with the historical facts that victims lasted for several days and that when Jesus died in only a few hours, Pilate was shocked. Besides, when Jesus uttered his last

The Passion of Jesus

words, he shouted, "It is finished!" It is quite impossible for someone who is suffocating to shout.

So why did Jesus die? Well, John 19:34 observes that the soldiers chose to lance Jesus' side rather than break his legs. When they did, blood and water flowed from his chest cavity. Because corpses don't bleed, the only blood that would have flowed is that drawn out by gravity. Unless the heart had ruptured, there would not have been a noticeable amount. Hence, it is most likely that Jesus died of a coronary rupture. Literally, Jesus died of a broken heart.

But that really only gets at the "how?" question, not the "why?" question. Why did Jesus die? First Corinthians 5:21 says, "God made him who knew no sin to become sin for us that we might become the righteousness of God." Now that *is* an amazing statement. Somehow Jesus, who had incarnated deity in his flesh, now incarnated the depravity of humanity. I know, it's too much to wrap your brain around—God became man and then became sin, so that, when he died, he could take our punishment with him. It is just too unbelievable, yet our faith rests upon it. But don't miss the second half. True enough, Jesus became sin on the cross. Yet there's more: we became righteousness through the cross. Because of Jesus' death, we have life—he took our sin and shame. To be sure, Jesus doesn't look like sin anymore than we look like God's righteousness. But that's because we are looking at it with eyes of flesh. We can only see the transient tangible with these eyes. We need to have God's perspective, we need to believe, we need to receive what Jesus has done for us and live lives free and alive and beautiful.

Pursuing the Passion of Jesus

Read and reflect on Psalm 22.

The Death of Life

THE DEATH OF DEATH

Our Lord has written the promise
of the resurrection,
not in books alone,
but in every leaf in springtime.
—Martin Luther

The resurrection is a fact of history
without which history
does not make sense.
—Clark H. Pinnock

Text: Luke 24:1-43   Memory: Luke 24:37-39

Misunderstood Messages   General Wellington command-
ed the victorious forces at the
great battle of Waterloo that effectively ended the Napoleonic
wars. The story has been told that when the battle was over,
General Wellington sent the great news of his victory to
England. A series of stations, one within sight of the next, had
been established to send the coded messages between
England and the European continent. The message to be sent
was "Wellington defeated Napoleon at Waterloo." Meanwhile
a fog set in and interrupted the message sending process. As
a result, people only saw news of "Wellington defeated—"
People in England were worried, scared, and saddened by the
news. Later, the fog cleared and the full message continued,
which was quite different from the outcome that the people
originally thought had happened.

The same was true on a Friday a few thousands years ago. But when Sunday rolled around, the message dramatically changed from "defeated" to "victorious."

Overview of the Text

Luke is one of those outsiders who, for some reason, joined the church. We must remember that this was when the church was still primarily Jewish, and "Gentiles" were considered unclean by the Hebrews. What made him join a group that heretofore had been at odds with the likes of Luke? Well, according to Luke's own presentation, both here and in the book of Acts, it was the bodily resurrection of Jesus of Nazareth. That's what drew him in. Now, some may say, "Oh that's just some archaic superstition." Granted, the ancients had their fair share of superstitions (as do we, if we're honest). But even in a first-century third-world country they knew people didn't rise from the dead. (Although the Jews believed in resurrection, it was specifically when all "good" people would raise at the end of time—like Christians believe today—not an individual raising from the dead in *this* space and time.) How much more would Luke have known this. He was a physician that dealt daily with the hard facts of concrete reality. Despite his best efforts, all his old patients stayed dead; how could he come to believe that his new Lord didn't? That's what he's about to tell us.

Pondering the Passion of Jesus

✳ In what ways do you identify with Luke?
✳ Is there an element of the resurrection story that still baffles you today? If so, which part?
✳ If you had lived in that day, what evidence would you have needed to convince you that Jesus really did rise from the dead?
✳ What excites you about your resurrection from the dead?

The Death of Death

64 Meaning of the Text Luke is one of the most interesting authors of the Bible. He is the only non-Jewish writer and perhaps the best of all historians. He is clearly familiar with Greco-Roman literature as well as Hebrew idioms. His vocabulary is huge (as is fitting for a well-traveled physician). He was a personal friend and traveling companion of Paul. So much more could be said but this suffices to show that Luke is no gullible ancient easily duped by fairy tales or superstitions. As a doctor, he has been thoroughly convinced in the reality of the bodily resurrection of Jesus because of what he calls "incontrovertible evidence" (Acts 1:3). So what was it that so convinced him?

1. Reliable Witnesses—If someone is taken to court, the prosecution brings forth evidence to convict them. Key to the argument would be reliable witnesses, especially those who could say, "Yes, we were there and we saw what happened." Generally just one witness isn't enough to secure a conviction. "Her word/his word" usually doesn't get you very far. If, however, two or three eyewitnesses agree in their testimony, then the case begins to mount. Let's apply those same rules of jurisprudence to the case of Christ.

Luke mentions three groups that gave testimony to Jesus. First we have some women who went to the tomb to pay their respects. What is interesting is that in those days women were not legal witnesses. Even if they wanted to, they couldn't testify in court for Jesus. So they aren't very good witnesses in their own day, but they serve as excellent witness in ours. Here's why: A number of scholars have suggested that Jesus didn't really raise from the dead bodily. Rather this was a story that developed over time and finally came to be believed as fact. This is the sort of blather one hears on PBS specials and reads in *Newsweek*. There are a number of problems with this theory (e.g., the Apostles' dying for their faith that had not yet developed; the very early institution of the Lord's Supper and baptism apart from the reality of the resurrection; the development of the church without its cornerstone tenet, the empty tomb; etc.). One of the most perplexing problems, however, are the women. If the resurrection was simply a story made up to exalt Jesus, then its author is indeed creative but really quite stupid. First of all, the "story" of the resurrection lacks one key element—the event of the resurrection itself—it is never described. Furthermore, the first witnesses are women whose opinions no one respects, even among the inner band! (Cf. Luke 24:11). Thus these women stand as inadvertent witnesses to the authenticity of this account.

The second witnesses are a pair on the road to Emmaus. Cleopas is named, his partner remains anonymous. Hopes dashed, they begin their sullen return to their home, some seven miles outside the Holy City. Suddenly Jesus joins them and inquires about their consternation. Well, you know the rest of the story: He walks and talks, they listen wide-eyed with hearts pounding in their chests. Finally, inside the house a veil is lifted from their eyes when he breaks bread and prays. Just at their flash point Jesus disappears as suddenly as he had joined them. What is interesting about this event is that they do not expect it. As we mentioned before, no Jew believed in an individual rising from the dead, only the resurrection of the nation at the end of time. Their *disbelief* lends credibility to their story. This isn't something invented. This isn't some subconscious desire wrestled into fictitious existence.

What's more, the movement was dead. On Friday afternoon Christianity was buried with a Nazarene corpse. Fact: No Messianic movement ever survived the death of its founder(s). In other words, so goes the Messiah, so goes the movement. This was especially true for Jesus. He was captured by the Romans he was "supposed to" conquer. He was shamefully executed after being betrayed by one of his own. What we expect to see is the inner band hunkered down behind locked doors and the faithful followers dispersed to

The Death of Death

their homes. Hello! That's exactly what happened. Without a colossal event to turn the tide, the Jesus movement would have disappeared into oblivion.

The third group we observe are the Apostles. One point should be made here. These are not nebulous, unidentified figures anymore than the other two groups. With the exception of Cleopas' traveling companion, all these witnesses have names. They could be interviewed, questioned, and investigated—put on the stand, so to speak (cf. Luke 1:1-4). In fact, Paul says there were nearly 500 still alive around A.D. 58 when he wrote 1 Corinthians (15:6) who could be questioned about the reality of this event. The Apostles especially were known, interrogated, and observed. One might say, "Oh, they stole the body and made up the story." Really?! And pray tell, why? Why steal the body when it would defile you and dishonor the one you loved? Why move the body when Jesus received the most honorable type of burial he could have been given? Why risk death by the guards when there's nothing to gain? Why make up a story you don't even believe in? Why continue a movement when all the followers have already gone home? Why follow the dangerous path of a murdered leader who failed to accomplish what you thought were his goals? And most importantly, why would all of the Apostles (save John) die a martyr's death for what they knew to be a lie?

Remember, we're not talking about men who wanted to foist a colossal prank on the world. Their character is clearly seen in their writings of the New Testament. Their integrity, sacrifice, and economic abandonment speaks for itself. They had everything to lose and nothing to gain in this world if Jesus really didn't raise from the dead. In fact, most of them fought the reality even when it was presented to them by the women, by Cleopas, or even by Jesus himself (cf. Luke 24:40-43). The fact is, they didn't *want* to believe in the resurrection and resisted it until the hard, cold (or in this case "warm") facts were undeniable.

Something of immense magnitude turned Peter from a coward intimidated by a girl at the gate to a bold proclaimer in the portico of Solomon just fifty days later. Something huge altered doubting Thomas. What is big enough to make James (Jesus' half-brother) turn from a mocking doubter (John 7:1-3), into a staunch leader of the Jerusalem church? And who can forget the 180° turn of Paul? The transformation of Jesus' inner band is a striking testimony to the reality of this event.

2. Physical Evidence—A second key element of any case is physical evidence. While we obviously don't have a body, there are some things we *do* have that would build a strong circumstantial case. First, Jesus showed his disciples his body (Luke 24:40). They saw the scars, they even laid hands on him (1 John 1:1-3). Initially even this didn't dispel their unbelief. So he ate a piece of broiled fish (Luke 24:41-43). This was no ghost nor some figment of their imaginations. He was for real!

A second bit of physical evidence is the empty tomb. Granted, archaeologists can't even agree on which site is the authentic burial place of Jesus. But isn't that the point? Every founder of a major world religion has a shrine commemorating the place of his/her burial. It is an inescapable human impulse to honor the remains of our greatest religious leaders. The fact that there is no shrine, no obelisk, nor any tomb that can be identified strongly suggests that there isn't one available!

Third, we have a couple of institutions in the Christian Church that go back to its inception—the Eucharist and Baptism. Can you imagine either of these getting off the ground without the bodily resurrection of Jesus? Into what would you baptize someone? Jesus' death?! Without the resurrection the act of Baptism might be a very effective means of curbing Christians' sin but not so helpful for church growth. And can you imagine how Communion would have gotten started? A group of guys are sitting around thinking

The Death of Death

they need to honor Jesus. One of them says, "Say, remember at the feeding of the 5,000 he said to eat his flesh and drink his blood?" (John 6:54). "Why don't we pretend that we are eating his rotting corpse?!" What a thought! Perhaps this would happen in some twisted Goth cult group, but we're talking about Kosher Jews here.

Given both the witnesses available and the physical evidence at hand, no wonder Luke the physician concluded with Paul the persecutor-turned-persecuted that Christ indeed has risen from the dead. And that changes everything!

Pursuing the Passion of Jesus

Check out **www.gospelcom.net/rzim** (Ravi Zacharias Ministries) & **www.josh.org** (Josh McDowell Ministries) for more information on the resurrection of Jesus.

> The stone at the tomb of Jesus was a pebble to the Rock of Ages inside.
> —Fred Beck
>
> The Gospels do not explain the resurrection; the resurrection explains the Gospels. Belief in the resurrection is not an appendage to the Christian faith; it is the Christian faith.
> —John S. Whale

THE BIRTH OF BELIEF

Text: John 20:19–21:19   **Memory:** John 20:26-29

Take the Son Years ago, a wealthy man and his only son shared a passion for art collecting. Together they traveled around the world adding only the finest works of art to their collection. Works by the likes of Van Gogh and Monet and Picasso adorned the walls of their family estate. The father looked on with satisfaction and pride as his son became an experienced collector.

Winter came and with it a letter from the government drafting the son to serve in a nearby war. The son left to serve his country, and the father was left to hope and pray for the best. The father's worst nightmares became a reality when he received a telegram stating that his son had been killed in action. The father faced the upcoming Christmas season alone, and the paintings on the wall only reminded him that his son wouldn't be coming home for Christmas.

70   Christmas morning arrived and with it a knock on the door. The father climbed out of his chair, opened the front door, and to his surprise there stood a young man dressed in military attire. The soldier introduced himself and said, "I knew your son, and he spoke often of your passion for art collecting. I have something here I would like to give you. May I come in?"

The father gladly welcomed the young man into his home. They exchanged pleasantries and the young man finally said, "I'm an artist and I've painted something for you." He handed the father a large package. Excitedly the old man tore into its brown paper wrapping and it gave way to reveal a portrait of his son in striking detail. It was no work of an artistic genius, no masterpiece by anyone's stretch of the imagination, but it didn't have to be. The father removed countless works of art from the walls and hung this portrait of his son for all to see.

Years passed and the father passed away as well. There was to be an auction of his personal belongings. Museum representatives and art critics and enthusiasts from all over the world gathered, hoping to bid on a priceless work of art. The auctioneer placed the first painting on the easel and asked for an opening bid. It was the painting of the old man's son. A few people laughed, most looked at one another and shrugged their shoulders. Finally someone shouted out, "C'mon, we didn't travel halfway around the world to bid on some painting of an old man's son! Let's get on with it!" But the auctioneer stood patiently, ignoring the crowd's disdain. And just when the tension in the room started to rise, a man in the back of the room stepped forward and said, "I'll take it! I'm the gardener at the estate. I knew the boy well, and it would be an honor to have it." His clothes were torn and dirty; he didn't fit in with the elite crowd that had gathered. He told the auctioneer, "I don't have any money to offer you. All I bring to the table is that I will take care of the painting."

The Passion of Jesus

The auctioneer raised his gavel and said, "Sold to the man in
the back!" The gardener nervously came out of the shadows
to claim his painting.

As he was taking it from the easel, the auctioneer raised
and dropped his gavel a second time. This time, announcing
that the auction was over. A stunned crowd sat in silent disbelief. Again someone shouted out, "How can this be? There
are millions of dollars of artwork to be bid on. How can the
auction be over?" The auctioneer smiled and said, "It's quite
simple. You see according to the will of the father, whoever
takes the son, takes it all!"

Overview of the Text In the last lesson we dealt with the
evidences for believing the resur-
rection. In this one we want to investigate its effects. What
happens when someone believes that Jesus did, in fact, rise
from the dead? Well, probably a thousand different things
with each individual. Nonetheless, we can probably narrow
our search a bit. Let's take a look at two towering figures in
the biblical narrative: Thomas and Peter. As we watch their
personal transformation, we will see a couple of key "resurrection" themes arise that will, in many ways, mirror our own
experience with the risen Christ.

Pondering the Passion of Jesus

* ✗ Are you a person who easily doubts or a person who
  easily believes? Choose one and explain why.
* ✗ Does failure consume you? Are you able to move on
  from poor choices, or do you wrestle with your con-
  science when you lay your head to the pillow at night?
* ✗ Have you taken your past and recycled it for good?
  Are you walking alongside people who have made
  similar choices in life, helping them see that grace
  abounds? Or are you keeping your past a secret,
  afraid of the embarrassment it might cause?

The Birth of Belief

72 **Meaning of the Text**

book:

We begin in the middle of our text. Here John states his purpose for the

> "Jesus did many other miraculous signs in the presence of his disciples, which are not recorded in this book. But these are written that you may believe that Jesus is the Christ, the Son of God, and that by believing you may have life in his name" (John 20:30-31).

Simply put, Jesus performed his miracles, climaxed by the resurrection, so that we would believe and through his name have abundant life. This statement is sandwiched between our two towering figures. On the front side is Thomas. He illustrates how one comes to *believe*. On the backside is Peter. He shows how one *receives* abundant life.

We're not told where he was that fateful night, but Thomas missed the grand entrance of the resurrected Christ. It was one of those electric moments. The two from Emmaus returned to the upper room, panting from a seven-mile sprint (cf. Luke 24:13). Their story sparks a flurry of excited testimonies as well as a few skeptical objections. In the midst of this flurry of words Jesus joins them with a simple statement: "Peace be with you." The greeting was common enough—it was echoed a thousand times a day in the market. But in this context it could have stopped a freight train. The room stood still in paralyzed silence. Jesus stretched out his nail-scarred hands and lifted his toga to reveal his gouged torso. Jubilation erupted.

Jesus' very breath blessed them with a symbolic promise of the coming Holy Spirit (John 20:21-23). Then, apparently, he leaves. The details are too sketchy to satisfy our flaming curiosity. Nonetheless, we can know that Jesus left before Thomas returned. He was the only one gone, perhaps taking up Iscariot's role as treasurer and going out for some supplies. His return is met by a barrage of animated explanations of what he'd missed. They talked about the two from Emmaus, the broiled fish, even the scars of the Master.

The Passion of Jesus

Thomas would have none of it. For him, seeing was believing and he told them as much. His dreams had been dashed. He'll not allow some gullible superstition to rebuild them only to have them crushed again.

Let's be clear about one thing. Thomas did believe in Jesus, so much so that he was willing to die as a martyr for the cause of the kingdom. Remember his words when Jesus called the boys to follow him to Bethany to raise Lazarus? "Let us also go, that we may die with him" (John 11:16). Thomas lacks neither courage nor devotion. His problem is perception. His faith rested in his eyes rather than his ears. His belief would be based on the tangible rather than trustworthy testimony and frankly, that's a problem.

A week later Jesus shows up again—same song, second verse, only this time Thomas is in the choir. Jesus saunters up to him and says, "Put your finger here; see my hands. Reach out your hand and put it into my side. Stop doubting and believe." There are a couple of interesting things about this statement. First, Jesus is quoting directly from Thomas' objections a week earlier: "Unless I put my finger in his hands where the nails were and put my fist in his side I will not believe." Thomas didn't *see* him so assumed he wasn't there. Jesus' quotation proves that he was. Whether we see him or not, whether we "feel" him or not, Jesus is very much present and very much aware of our struggle to follow him.

A second interesting thing is Jesus' statement, "stop doubting." From this Thomas received the title "Doubting Thomas." It's kind of a bum rap really, since none of the other disciples (save John [John 20:8]), ever believed before seeing Jesus in person. The point is, this story of Thomas represents the whole group, and often ourselves. We tend to seek the tangible rather than believing the testimony. That's the point of this story. Jesus concludes by saying, "Because you have seen me, you have believed; blessed are those who have not seen and yet have believed." The most powerful faith is not

The Birth of Belief

based on what the eyes can see but what the heart can believe through the reliable witness of the Apostles, the prophets, the Scriptures, even the Holy Spirit. The eyes are easily manipulated, tricked with sleight of hand; but reliable testimony stands the test of time.

One more tidbit before moving on to Peter. Thomas makes a most extraordinary statement about Jesus: "My Lord and my God." Now, many a Jew had said to another man, "My Lord." After all, they were a nation enslaved many times. But never had a Jew said to another man, "My God." Oh, the Romans pretended their emperors were divine as did the Egyptians their pharaohs and the Babylonians their kings. But this was something strikingly different for a Jew. The resurrection so totally transformed this skeptic that he went from resistant doubt to full confession in an instant.

So there stands Thomas with a declaration of deity still dripping from his lips. He believes. But there are many who stand at a distance from the Christ, not because of Thomas's doubt, but due to Peter's failure. Can you see him in the shadows of the courtyard. Some "rock." Jesus predicted his failure and Peter had the audacity to argue with him! "Even if all the others deny you, Lord, I never will!" (Matt. 26:33-34). Oh, there's nothing wrong with his *intentions*. He even had the nerve to launch an attack on 600 soldiers with two swords and a Jesus in his hip pocket. Nonetheless, before that fateful cock crowed, he had fulfilled his dark destiny. In fact, who, besides Peter, looks more like Judas?

As we head to the north shore of the lake in John 21, we see Peter back in the boat. There's nothing *morally* wrong with that, I suppose, after all, one does have to make a living. Nonetheless, it seems sadly symbolic. He's back at ground zero where Jesus found him some three years ago.

For Peter these appearances had to be a mixed blessing. On the one hand, Peter really did adore Jesus. Their hearts had been woven together over the past three years. On the

The Passion of Jesus

other hand, he had proven a turncoat. What place would a man like that ever have in Jesus' new government? What could he possibly do?

After breakfast, and, of course, an incredible catch that reminds Peter of who Jesus is, it's time for Jesus to remind Peter who *he* is. The Lord invites him on a walk; the others trail behind at a respectable distance. Jesus asks, "Peter, do you love me?" How those words must have pierced his soul. "Yes, Lord, you know that I love you." "Okay, then," said Jesus, "Feed my sheep." With a heart pounding heavier than his feet on those dusty roads, Peter takes a few more breathless steps. Jesus asks the same question a second time. The responses are the same although his face is surely a bit more flushed. Perhaps he looks over his shoulder to see how close the others are and just how much they heard. To his consternation, John is taking it all in. A few more steps then a third time the same question pummels his soul. The question would stop here. Perhaps it would have been easier if Jesus asked just once more. But there it stands: One question for each time Peter denied Jesus. The flashbacks were blinding.

Yet through this painful reminder is a deep kindness. Jesus had given Peter back the keys. He was still the shepherd. Failure, even of an egregious variety, doesn't remove the call of God on one's life. Peter had lost his footing, his dignity, his arrogance, and one day he would even lose his independence (John 21:18-19), but he hadn't lost Jesus. Or perhaps we should say, Jesus hadn't lost him. Nor has he lost you. Perhaps it's time for you to get out of the courtyard and get on to the north shore of the lake. There is a Lord waiting for you. His call hasn't been destroyed with your disobedience. It's time to get on with the business of feeding sheep. Just as Thomas teaches us how to believe, so Peter teaches us how to persevere. The resurrection is the power of both and whoever follows the Son, whoever is humble enough to admit failure and rebound, whoever takes the Son, takes it all!

The Birth of Belief

Start a support group in your church. Begin with one. Choose a specific area of pain or problem (divorce, alcohol or drug abuse, pornography, sexual abuse, etc.). Find a stable person to facilitate the group, establish guidelines of accountability and confidentiality, and determine a course of recovery for hurting people. You'll be amazed at how true community with honest dialogue will change the atmosphere of your church and the course of your own life.

12　　　　**12**

ON YOUR MARK, GET SET, GO!!!

12　　　　**12**

> Do not pray for easy lives;
> pray to be stronger people.
> Do not pray for tasks equal
> to your powers; pray for
> powers equal to your tasks.
> Then the doing of your work
> shall be no miracle,
> but you shall be a miracle.
> Every day you shall wonder
> at the richness of life which has
> come to you by the grace of God.
>
> —Phillips Brooks

Text: Mark 16:15-18 　　　　 **Memory:** Mark 16:15

Cultural Squeamishness

Scott and I had been asked to preach at a church in a remote mountain area of Haiti known as Lariye. It was a good hike from the city we were living in, but both of us anticipated a great weekend of teaching and fellowship. When we arrived, we set our things down and were led to a small open-air building that served as a village church. As the sun set, people began to gather. A room that should've seated just a few people was crammed with people. Some sat on makeshift benches, others stood, but no one seemed to complain.

That evening, we both preached and after the service were taken to a thatched roof hut that would serve as our haven of rest for the weekend. Out of curiosity, a number of the people watched us unpack our belongings and get ready for bed. As I was spraying down with bug repellent, the owner of the home, an elderly Haitian man, walked in and laughed. It wasn't uncommon for Haitians to laugh at a tall, skinny white kid with his shirt off, but his laugh had a different ring to it. He smiled at me and said, "You won't be needing that up here." My immediate thought was, "Great! No mosquitoes at this elevation means I might just get my first good night's sleep in a long time." My hope was short lived! As he left the hut, he turned around and said, "We don't have mosquitoes, we have rats!" Scott looked at me and we didn't know if we should laugh or cry! Crying seemed more appropriate.

We laid down, turned off our flashlights and as we did, we could hear what sounded like Jolly the Green Giant stepping on a bag of Ruffles above our heads! We quickly turned our lights back on only to be greeted by hundreds of little eyes. Rats! Everywhere! They used us as a major highway between their feeding grounds and nests. And worse, they also saw us as a public restroom! Needless to say, we didn't sleep at all.

The following day, we taught on a variety of subjects and were fed only one meal. Tired and hungry, we ate what was placed in front of us. It wasn't rats, but it wasn't much better! That night, we preached again, and it's one thing when you sleep through someone's sermon, it's a whole new ball game when you sleep through one of your own! To this day, I don't know that I said anything coherent that night.

When we arrived back at our hut, we both decided that we couldn't spend another sleepless night with the rats so we went outside and fell asleep on the ground. Within minutes of doing so, I felt Scott shaking me saying, "Jon, it's raining. We better move back inside." God has a good sense of humor! We spent yet another night with the rats.

The following morning was Sunday and we once again found ourselves in front of a congregation of people hungry for more of God's Word. To our surprise, five people came forward to accept Christ. A crowd gathered outside and we began what would be a two-hour journey to the nearest watering hole. The people sang and laughed and encouraged one another as we walked up one hill and down another. And I'll never forget turning the last corner and seeing the river where we would be baptizing people. Animals were bathing in it, people were doing their laundry in it. There is no nice way to put this: it resembled a sewer, not a river. But I wish I could describe the look on those people's faces as they came up out of that dirty water as spiritually clean people. As I embraced each one of them, I realized they didn't have a care in the world! They weren't concerned about dirty river water, long walks, standing in church, and even living with rats. In the midst of terrible surroundings and fatigue, my eyes were opened up to see what really counts: people need Jesus.

And when we follow him and obey him, he shows up!

Overview of the Text This is a funky text. You have snake-handling, speaking in tongues, and shots of strychnine all to the glory of God! What are we supposed to make of this? Well, this text certainly stands out but it need not stand alone. After all, this is only one of five great commission texts. Perhaps by placing it next to its kissin' cousins their relationship can shed some light on the meaning of these strange words.

Pondering the Passion of Jesus

⚕ Have you been on a short-term missions trip? If so, describe your experience.

⚕ Are you supporting missionaries through prayer and with your finances? If so, describe the mission. If not, we strongly encourage you to start today!

⚕ Does your church have a strategic missions program? Are you simply meeting physical needs or are you addressing deep-rooted spiritual needs in the countries you are targeting?

On Your Mark, Get Set, GO!!!

✷ Do you ever catch yourself doing ministry by human ability as opposed to relying on the power of God? What do you do to correct the situation?

Meaning of the Text   I'm not sure anyone likes everything in this text. Oh, we all pretty much agree that verse 15 is cool—you know, going into all the world and making disciples. After all, these do appear to be Jesus' last words, his final, great commission to his followers. As for verse 16, that's somewhat problematic for many Evangelicals who trumpet "Faith Only." You see, baptism stands right next to faith when it comes to salvation—a little too close for Calvinistic comfort. It's just kind of messy when packaged with a faith-only theology. Of course, the discomfort with verse 16 is nothing compared to verses 17-18. Well, actually, verse 17 is not so bad since we can locate it in the book of Acts. At least the non-Pentecostals could say that's what happened a long time ago but has little relevance for us today. That's one way to be done with it. But verse 18 . . . what in the world is going on with the serpents and strychnine?! Whose bright idea was that?

Okay, so this is a difficult text. What are we going to do with it? Well, some have simply dismissed it as inauthentic. The more modern translations of the Bible (NIV, NASB, RSV) have all placed it in brackets, indicating that some of the earliest and best manuscripts do not include it. While that is true, it is also somewhat misleading. First, it is included in some old manuscripts, and even those that do not include it often leave a space for it or place some kind of note in the text suggesting something curious is going on here. Second, if we simply drop it, then Mark ends at verse 8 with these awkward words: "Trembling and bewildered, the women went out and fled from the tomb. They said nothing to anyone, because they were afraid." That's kind of an anticlimactic end to a gospel of "good news"! Third, while this text is very different ending had enough authenticity that the early church respectfully accepted it as a conclusion to the book.

Let me be clear on two points. One, this is a problematic passage both textually and theologically. Two, the early church still respected and used it for 1500 years before we came along. Perhaps we should take more than a surface glance at it before dismissing it. I suggest we do that in two ways: By placing it in its cultural setting of the first century and by placing it beside the other commission accounts.

Mark 16:15-18 in Cultural Context

When we read about snake handling and strychnine we tend to picture radical backwoods preachers of the Appalachian mountains with poor, uneducated congregants. For them these things are a test of faith, for visitors they are a circus side-show. The PBS specials draw us to the edge of the couch as we watch with mouth agape at ﹁some "elder" caressing a handful of poisonous serpents. They dance and shout, moan and wail in a state of religious ecstasy. We shake our heads and say, "That's just nuts!"

For the Christians of the early church, however, snakes were never part of the church service. They were, however, often associated with evangelism. You see, serpents were one of the deadly animals used for executions, especially in the arena. They were right up there with lions, bears, and packs of wild dogs. Likewise, poison was one of the ways people were assassinated along with swords, stones, and ropes. What we have here is not a test of faith (or fate), but a pagan's response to preaching. In short, as Christians carried out verses 15-16, pagans responded with verse 18. More to the point, when Christians carry out God's commission, God himself participates through miraculous intervention. Sometimes it was through tongues and exorcism which gave cre-

82 dence to the preaching. Sometimes it was through miraculous release from lethal opposition. But in all situations, God showed up when "air support" was necessary to carry out the mission assigned to the church.

Does this mean that Christians never died in the line of duty? No, of course not. But it does mean that, when the church is the church, God will be God. When we do what he has asked us to do (vv. 15-16), he will support us in ways that only God can (vv. 17-18).

Mark 16:15-18 in Literary Context

This strange text is only one of five great commission texts (cf. Matt. 28:18-20; Luke 24:46-49; John 20:21-23; Acts 1:8). Each of these texts is unique in some way. All of them, however, have two common elements: the task of evangelism assigned to the church and God's promise of his continued presence. We have already noticed from Mark 16 how God promised to "show up" when the church needed him to accomplish the great commission. Now let's look at Matthew's rendition.

As Jesus stands on a mountain, stunned disciples surrounding him, he gives his final marching orders: Go and make disciples. How do we do that? Well, we baptize them *into* Christ and then teach them to *grow up* in Christ. That's simple enough . . . until we hear that we are to do this globally, not merely in the local village! How on earth (pun intended) can we go global with this little enterprise? How can we win the world to Jesus? It may not be easy, but it is simple—Jesus joins us even "unto the end of the age." We can't do this alone. Yet with his promised support, this is a reasonable order.

Both Luke and John place Jesus in the upper room, commissioning his disciples to take this message of repentance and forgiveness to all nations (Luke 24:47). Remember, these

guys *barely* believe Jesus has risen (in fact, Thomas isn't even
on board yet). They are still hunkered down in an upper
room, scared to death some Roman soldier will stumble
across them. They're not fit for such a daunting task . . .
they're daunted! What hope do they have? Well, in both Luke
and John, Jesus bestows on them the promise of the Holy
Spirit (Luke 24:49; John 20:22; cf. Acts 1:8). The Spirit will
supply the power they require, the courage they lack, the wis-
dom they need, even the very words to speak in the face of
imposing opposition. Never fear, the Spirit is here.

Now, let's look at these together. Mark suggests that if
the church is the church, then God will be God—he will show
up with the miraculous intervention needed to face certain
persecution. Matthew quotes Jesus who promises to accom-
pany the disciples to the four corners of the earth as they
baptize converts and establish churches. Luke and John tag-
team to tell of Jesus' promise of the abiding Holy Spirit. Place
all four Gospels' commissions side by side and you see the
entire Trinity standing behind it.

What can we make of this? The great commission is
God's purpose for the church. He will support it with all his
resources. It may be *our* commission, but it is *his* mission! Our
goal is not the building of buildings, the perpetuation of pro-
grams, the raising of funds, social awareness, education, pol-
itics, family values, moral media, or a hundred other noble
pursuits. Our primary directive is to preach the good news of
Jesus Christ to every people group on the planet. And if we
will, then the entire Trinity is at our disposal.

Are you interested in a deeper relationship with Jesus?
Preach the Gospel and he'll show up! Have you ever wanted
to watch God do a miracle, I mean a *bona fide* wonder? Make
disciples and watch what happens. Have you ever pleaded
with God for more of his Holy Spirit—to guide you, teach you,
empower you, strengthen you? Well, then get on with the
task. Our great God is more eager for these things than you

On Your Mark, Get Set, GO!!!

are, I can assure you of this. He's waiting expectantly for you to take up the task . . . then He'll show up in all his fullness and wonder.

Pursuing the Passion of Jesus

Open your home up to missionaries. When you hear that someone is returning from work on foreign soil, make your home and possessions available to them. Loan them a car, provide meals or money for meals, and even match the money you set aside for personal vacation with equal monies to send them on a vacation. And when they return to the field, pray for them, write them, send them care packages, visit them, and keep a picture in your home of them for your children to see. Attend missions conferences, read missionary biographies, read daily newspapers so you know what is happening in the world today, and most of all, be open to the call of God in your life to be a servant/guest on foreign soil. We've all been called to "go," so if you stay, you better have a calling not to "go."

BACK WHERE HE BELONGS

> The sky is
> the daily bread
> of the eyes.
> —Ralph Waldo Emerson

Text: Luke 24:50-51; Acts 1:9-11   **Memory:** Acts 1:10-11

A Messenger from Beyond

Roald Amundsen, the great Norwegian explorer, was the first to discover the magnetic meridian of the North Pole and was the first man to discover the South Pole. On one of his trips, Amundsen took a homing pigeon with him. When he had finally reached the top of the world, he opened the bird's cage and set it free.

Imagine the delight of Amundsen's wife, back in Norway, when she looked up from the doorway of her home and saw the pigeon circling in the sky above. No doubt she exclaimed, "He's alive! My husband is still alive!"

So it was when Jesus ascended. He was gone, but the disciples clung to his promise to send them the Holy Spirit. What joy must have been theirs when the Holy Spirit descended on them at Pentecost.

Overview of the Text

Only Luke describes the ascension. Oh sure, Mark 16:19 has that little snippet about it, but there's not enough there to hang your theological hat on. We're left with one clear description, although Luke gives it twice (Luke 24:50-51 and Acts 1:9-11). Frankly, it sounds like a fairy tale—as Jesus was talking he just started floating away, leaving the disciples staring into the sky like children who lost a helium balloon. For many the ascension is just more comfortable to ignore than explain. That, however, is a mistake. For this curious event is the crowning glory of the Life of Christ and part and parcel with the resurrection. It is a promise for each believer which stands on the same sure ground as Jesus' deity, death, and resurrection. Our aim here is to show this event was predicted in the OT, assumed in the NT, and is of critical significance for believers.

Pondering the Passion of Jesus

- ☧ Have you ever wanted to fly, or are you afraid of heights?
- ☧ If you had been on that hillside the day Jesus ascended, what would've been your response?
- ☧ Do you think Jesus missed the disciples?

Meaning of the Text

> The LORD says to my Lord:
> "Sit at my right hand
> until I make your enemies
> a footstool for your feet" (Ps. 110:1).

This is the most commonly cited quotation of all the Old Testament, and it is a direct claim for the ascension. The Bible never assumes simply that Jesus would be restored to life, but that he would be restored to his rightful place at God's right hand. Theologically speaking, the ascension and the resurrection are two sides of the same coin that vindicate Jesus as the Son of God. You wouldn't have one without the other.

Thus, the ascension is *assumed* throughout the NT even if it is only *described* by Luke. Fill out the chart below and you'll get a feel for how deeply ingrained the ascension is in the minds and hearts of NT authors:

NT Text	What does this teach about the ascension?
Luke 22:69	
John 20:17	
Acts 7:55	
Romans 8:34	
Ephesians 1:18-23	
Philippians 2:9-11	
Philippians 3:10, 20	
Colossians 3:1	
Hebrews 1:3	
Hebrews 8:1-2	
Hebrews 10:12-14	
1 Peter 3:21-22	

So far we've come to two conclusions. First, Jesus expected to return to the right hand of the Father. This was, in essence, the completion of the resurrection. He was not merely raised from the earth but to the very throne room of heaven. Second, the bulk of the NT authors assumed this to have taken place: Mark, Luke, John, Paul, the author of Hebrews, and Peter. The

Back Where He Belongs

fact is, Matthew is the *only* NT author to say nothing about it at all. So the fact that we have only one clear description is overshadowed by the overwhelming assumption of this event.

But why was this so important? Does it really matter that Jesus ascended? Yes, Yes, Yes! There are at least three reasons this event is crucial to Christians. First, the ascension marks the completion of Jesus' work on earth. We're not just saying the whistle blew and it was time for him to go home. We're suggesting that the ascension validated his life and death. It proves that Jesus was God's man and that what he did was effective, not merely on the human plane but also in the eyes of God. It confirms our confidence that our sins are forgiven and our heavenly hope is secure. What Jesus did on the cross was not for naught—it "worked" and we are thus saved (John 17:4,5; Phil. 2:6,9,10)

Second, when Jesus went away, it was a mission, not abandonment. He didn't go home to rest while leaving us to our own devices. He went to prepare a place for us (John 14:2). Even now he is diligently working on our behalf so that when he returns our eternal home will be secured.

Now we mustn't think of Jesus as a construction worker building heaven. I've heard people say that God spent seven days on this creation and look how wonderful it is. Yet Jesus has been working for 2,000 years on the New Heaven and the New Earth so it must be exponentially better than the first. That's a bit of literalistic nonsense. Jesus is preparing a place for us, not by building heaven, but by sitting beside his Father acting as our advocate (Rom. 8:34; Heb. 7:25). Even now, as we sin, Jesus goes to bat for us with the Eternal Judge. He takes upon himself our penalty and buries it deep in the atoning sacrifice of Calvary. Because he has already paid the price for our sins, he can plead for our release. *That* is his preparation for our eternity; through his advocacy we have a place with the Father forever.

Third, when Jesus went to be with the Father, he sent the Holy Spirit to be with us (John 16:7). While Jesus is on the job with God, the Holy Spirit works with us. He stands in for Jesus here on this earth. Essentially, all that Jesus did for the disciples while he walked these dusty roads, the Holy Spirit continues to do for every member of his global church. Jesus gave specific instructions to the disciples; so does the Holy Spirit (Acts 13:2,4; 15:28; 20:23; 21:11). Jesus taught them to know the mind of God; so does the Holy Spirit (1 Cor. 2:10-14). Jesus prepared them to preach; so does the Holy Spirit (Matt. 10:20; Mark 13:11; Luke 12:12). The Spirit of God gives wise counsel (John 14:16-17; 14:26; 15:26; 16:13-15), guides us in prayer (Rom. 8:26-27), and changes our hearts (Rom. 1:29; Gal. 3:14; Titus 3:5), our behavior (Rom. 7:6; 8:1-16; 2 Cor. 3:3,6,8; Gal. 3:2-3; 5:16-18; 5:25), and our affiliations (Rom. 8:16-17; Gal. 4:6). He grants us spiritual gifts (Rom. 12:6-8; 1 Cor. 12:4,7-12; Eph. 4:11-13), fruit (Gal. 5:22-23), and armament (Eph. 6:17-18). He does a dozen other things we're not able to address here. Suffice to say, however, that through the power of the Spirit we are enabled to live in this world as representatives of the living Christ. He guides us through confusion, encourages us through despair, strengthens us through opposition, empowers us for ministry. In short, through the Spirit of Christ, the body of Christ becomes the continuing incarnation of Christ until he returns.

The ascension is the crowing glory of the incarnation. As we bring this series of lessons to a close, we pray that you will live in light of the ascension. May you be a people of power because of the Spirit given after the ascension. May you be a people of hope because Christ, our advocate, is preparing a place for you at the Father's side. May you be a people of freedom and celebration because your sins have been forgiven, authenticated by the ascension. You see, the raising of Jesus was not merely a historical moment. It was an enacted promise. So goes Jesus, so go his people. As he was

Back Where He Belongs

raised, so also will we be. In fact, our spirits are already lifted to the very presence of God (Col. 3:3). And one day soon, our bodies will catch up.

Pursuing the Passion of Jesus

Make plans every spring to attend the Southeast Christian Church Easter Pageant in Louisville, Kentucky. Check out their web site for further information: www.southeastchristian.org. This event is more than worth your time! Tickets go fast, so plan ahead.

Acknowledgments

A special thanks to: Allison, Ava, my family, Archimel, Dana, Mike, TD, Scott, Bro, Monte, Tina, Susan, Mary Helen, Ashley, Ann, Gordon, Scott N., Tim, Dave, and Jessica S. Your love, encouragement, friendship, prayers, and proofreading have been a source of joy for me.

Jon

About the Authors

Mark Moore is Professor of New Testament at Ozark Christian College, teaching in the areas of Life of Christ, Acts, and Bible Interpretation. Mark did his undergraduate work at Ozark Christian College. He went on to earn a Masters in Education from Incarnate Word College in San Antonio, Texas, while pastoring a bilingual church there. Later he earned a Masters in Religious Studies from Southwest Missouri State University. He returned to Ozark to teach in the fall of 1990.

Mark is the author of a number of books, including other works on the Life of Christ: a two-volume set entitled *The Chronological Life of Christ*, and the more devotional *Encounters with Christ*. He is a popular speaker for both adult and youth conferences.

Mark makes his home in Joplin, Missouri, where his favorite place is with his wife, Barbara, and two teenage children, Josh and Megan, who both know and honor the Lord.

Jon Weece is currently ministering with Southland Christian Church in Lexington, Kentucky. He began in the summer of 2000 on the Teaching Team and as an Adult Discipleship Associate. Jon has served four years as a missionary in Haiti.

He graduated with a Bachelor of Biblical Literature degree from Ozark Christian College in Joplin, Missouri. He and his wife Allison live in Lexington. Jon is passionate about being a good husband and dad. He also enjoys a good Sunday afternoon drive, cooking steaks on the grill, reading a good book, and fishing.